Cookbook From Hell

A Prison Cookbook

by: Shane Cillessen

Cookbook From Hell

First Edition

A convict cookbook especially for inmates in
Colorado Prisons (Hell)

I created this cookbook for fellow inmates in Colorado prisons. It could be used in other states; however the available commissary there will surely be different. Some recipes were contributed by other inmates who shall remain anonymous. (you know who you are)

ISBN-13: 978-1-105-26534-1

Cookbook From Hell

Acknowledgments

First and foremost I thank God for rescuing me from myself and giving me another chance to live for Him. Ever since I accepted Him, I have been blessed. I may be in prison now, but I am truly blessed every day and every way. My family is doing fine out there under His watch. I have a great cellie, a good job where I am able to make a difference through Habitat for Humanity, and the opportunity to do things like this cookbook, completely unheard of in prison.

A project like this is impossible from inside these walls without a lot of help from outside. I am extremely grateful to all of those who made this possible. Especially my sister, Tara who actually did the publishing for me. Thank you sis!

I would like to thank those fellow inmates who shared their recipes and who broke bread with me during these years in prison.

I would also like to thank the following people outside, not only for helping me create some of the recipes here, but mostly for being there, for supporting me through my sentence despite the crimes I've committed. Your love and support are all I have now and I am eternally grateful for each one of you.

Mom and Dad
Sister - Tara
Grandma - Jackie
Grandma - Dorothy
Ex Wife - Heather
All my kids
Billy (BBL)
Dave and Gail
Pastor George
and all of the rest of my friends and family that didn't disown me.

Thank you all and God bless you!

Cookbook From Hell

Introduction

It may seem like hell being incarcerated, but try to remember, it can always be worse. At least we can still make half-edible food. That's right, and if you've never tried it, this book might just help you cope with hard times through better cuisine.

Most, if not all, chow halls serve straight garbage to us daily. With a little money on your books, or a "sugar daddy," you can eat better in your cell. Okay, okay, lets not get carried away… Prison is still prison, and these recipes wouldn't hold a candle to what you could eat out of the dumpster behind any restaurant outside these walls. But we can still make the best of what we've got. Don't trip though, I've been eating nothing but these recipes for several years and I'm killing my time just fine.

I have tailored most of these recipes for two people; you and your cellie, as most good cellies eat together and share the cost. However, you can cut most of these recipes in half, or add to them if you plan to make a spread with more people.

Commissary products change constantly making it difficult to get consistent quantities and retain exact recipes. Prison cooking is definitely not an exact science, but with a little skill and some patience, you would be amazed what you can accomplish with what is actually available to us.

I have included a few comments about prison life throughout this book, as well as some of my favorite quotes for your entertainment. I hope you get as much amusement reading this as I have - living in "Hell."

"Two roads diverged in the middle of my life. I took the road less traveled by and that's made all the difference.

Robert Frost

Table of Contents

Commissary List

For those who are not in prison, or not in Colorado, I will try to describe most of the commissary items used in these recipes so you can try to replicate the quantities shown.
As of December, 2011:

Com. #	Description	Quantity	Brand
2004	Lemonade Mix (Sweetened)	16 oz	Farmers Brothers
2015	Hot Cocoa Mix	16 oz	Farmers Brothers
2050	Tang	12 oz	Keefe
2065	Instant Tea Powder (makes 1 gal.)	.56 oz	Nestea
3005	Refried Beans (Dehydrated)	7 oz/1.5 cup	Fresh Start
3155	Chili with Beans	11.25 oz	Brushy Creek
3385	Mackerel Filets	5 oz	Fisherman's Paradise
3161	Mozzarella Cheese Stick	4 oz	City Cow
3162	Jalapeno Squeeze Cheese	2 oz	City Cow
3164	Cream Cheese	1 oz	Rondelé
3165	Cheddar Cheese Powder	1 lb	Farmers Brothers
3166	Black Bean Dip	7 oz/1.5 cup	Fresh Start
3167	Hot Garlic Chili Sauce	8 oz	Huy Fong
3168	Vegetable Flakes	1.25 oz	Spice Classics
3174	BBQ Sauce	18 oz	Home Brand
3175	Fritos Corn Chips	16 oz	Fritos
3205	Tostitos Tortilla Chips	16 oz	Tostitos
3215	Chocolate Chip Cookies	10 oz	Checkers Cookies
3220	Duplex Sandwich Cookies (14 ea)	5 oz	Basil
3225	Lemon Sandwich Cookies	5 oz	Basil
3250	Low Fat Cereal (Granola)	16 oz	Sunbelt
3275	Bagel	4 oz	Golden Valley
3280	Graham Crackers (3 Sleeves)	14.4 oz	Ralston
3295	Saltine Crackers (4 sleeves)	16 oz	Golden Valley
3320	Honey	12 oz	Fresh Start
3325	Marion Berry Jam	16 oz	Fresh Start
3327	White Rice (Instant)	7 oz /2.5 cup	Fresh Start
3328	Rolled Oats (Instant)	16 oz	Fresh Start

Approximate costs are included in most recipes and are accurate as of the time of publishing this cookbook. Prices change almost weekly and all prices are considering the actual partial quantities. Obviously if you need to buy a whole bag of powdered eggs to get 4 scoops, your initial cost will be higher. Once you have established stock of everything, your costs will even out.

Com. #	Description	Quantity	Brand
3340	Peanut Butter (Creamy)	18 oz	Food Express
3345	Sausage (Spicy Summer Sausage)	5 oz stick	Hometown
3347	Spam	3 oz	Single
3350	Jalapenos (pickled)	1-2 peppers	Tito's
3355	Lasagna	11.25 oz	Brushy Creek
3360	Pizza Kit (2 crusts & 2 sauce pks)	2 ea	Various
3363	Pepperoni (sliced)	3.5 oz	Back Country
3365	Taco Mix (soy - like 1 lb ground beef)	8 oz	Fresh Start
3370	Roast Beef in Gravy	11.25 oz	Brushy Creek
3395	Cherry Pie	4 oz	Little Debbie
3400	German Chocolate Cookie Rings (8)	8.3 oz	Little Debbie
3425	Nutty Bars (6)	12 oz	Little Debbie
3455	Chili Ramen	3 oz	Nissin Top Ramen
3480	Beef Stew (bag)	11.25 oz	Brushy Creek
3490	Sugar (individual packets)	70 packets	Varies
3500	Fast Mac & Cheese	3 oz	Velveeta
3505	Tortillas	1 dozen	Pesos Tortillas
3510	Tuna	4.23 oz	Fresh Catch
3513	Pink Salmon	6 oz	Chicken of the Sea
3515	White Chicken Chunks	4.5 oz	Brushy Creek
3520	Tilapia with Lemon & Pepper	3.53 oz	Fresh Catch
3610	Powdered Eggs (48 scoops=1 egg ea.)	6 oz	Egg Sense
3700	Diced Carrots (dehydrated)	3 oz	Harmony House
3710	Green Beans (dehydrated)	1.75 oz	Harmony House
3720	Chopped Onions (dehydrated)	2.25 oz	Harmony House
3730	R&G Peppers (dehydrated)	2.25 oz	Harmony House
3740	Diced Tomatoes (dehydrated)	2.25 oz	Harmony House
3800-03	Mustard, Ketchup, Hot Sauce, Mayo	12 packets	Squeeze-Ums

Prison Cooking Basics:

It is a different world cooking in prison. No refrigeration available means everything you make must be eaten right away. However "right away" means something entirely different in prison too. You can keep a few burritos in a plastic bag on the floor for up to 48 hours. You can use your window in the wintertime for a "refrigerator" when it is cold outside, but generally we just throw it on the floor. Everything we get on canteen is loaded with preservatives as it is all processed and or dehydrated food.

Prison cooking is usually done in the pod microwave, however if you are locked down, you can still cook in your coffee pot or hot pot. I use my coffee maker for most recipes anyway if only to make hot water to reconstitute the dehydrated beans and rice.

About measuring quantities… Since none of us actually have measuring spoons or cups, you'll have to do with what you've got. Our tumbler is 16 oz or 2 cups to the step just below the rim. Our coffee cup is 8 oz or 1 cup. Our bowl is 6.3 cups or 1.6 quarts. You can use any white spork to measure teaspoons and any large orange spork to measure tablespoons if you need to.

Snacks and Beverages

My Two Cents:

If I could give you one bit of advice, I would say "Never Take A Plea Deal!" Everyone has the right to a speedy trial (don't waive this!!!) that means the courts are required to hold your trial within 180 days of when you were charged. If everyone refused to take a plea, and took their case to trial, the courts would be so backed up they couldn't hear all the cases in time and most cases would be dismissed. Your cooperation is never rewarded, it is only taken advantage of! So make them work for your conviction! Remain silent, get a lawyer, and never waive any hearings or rights. Once you accept a plea bargain, you lose all rights to appeal and reconsideration. Let me say that again… If you enter a guilty plea to a plea bargain or otherwise, you lose your rights to appeal. So stay strong and fight for your rights!

I realize it is difficult to pass up a plea deal when you are facing some real time. In fact that's the game they play. They charge you with so many charges and threaten you with so much time that you buckle under the pressure. Been there. But if you keep your mouth shut and stay strong you will never regret it, and if everyone played the game the same way, they couldn't convict everyone.

If you are already in prison, my advice would be to do your own number. Don't let anyone put cables on you, and don't lay your shit on anyone else. We all have our problems and nobody wants to do your time too. If you wish to do the prison tattoo thing, be careful. Hep-C and HIV are rampant in prison, and write-ups are a bitch. Get your own needles and keep them for yourself. Another thing, don't join a gang just because you're scared. Gangs are a huge part of prison but they are weakened by those who don't truly belong. If you were a G on the outs, or you truly believe in the cause and wish to ride with a particular gang, that's different. If you are weak and cannot stand alone, you might fall into a gang but be careful what you fall for. Someone once said, "If you don't stand for something, you'll fall for anything." Stand for yourself first because at the end of the day, that's all you'll have in here. If you keep to yourself, and keep yourself busy, your time will go faster.

"Silence is a friend that will never betray you."
Chinese Proverb

Lets start simple. Your people can buy "Whole Enchilada" chip mix ready made on the gift pack, but you can make an even better chip mix using every day canteen chips.

Simple Chip Mix

Qty.	*Description*	*Commissary #*
1 bag	Nacho Cheese Tortilla Chips	3190
1 bag	Hot or Regular Corn Chips	3193
2 bags	Crunchy Cheese Puffs	3438
1 bag	Hot Cheese Puffs	3200
1/2 bag	Pretzels	3197

Approx Cost: $8.25 total

Mix everything together and enjoy. Makes a lot! Keep stored in original chip bags and seal with tape or ID clips.

Sometimes we can get Chex mix on the gift pack or around Christmas time. I like to make a spicy Fiddle Faddle with it.

Spicy Fiddle Faddle

Qty.	*Description*	*Commissary #*
2 bags	Chex Mix or Chex Cereal	Gift Pack
1 bag	Salted Peanuts	3050
6 tubs	Butter	Chow
1 tbsp	Garlic Chili Sauce	3167

Approx Cost: $6.00 total

Combine Chex Mix and peanuts in a couple bowls.
Melt butter in microwave about 20 sec. Add hot sauce and mix well. Add to Chex Mix and stir to coat evenly.
Store in original Chex Mix bags.

Variations:
You can add any cereal, crackers, bagel chips or whatever you like to make your own mix. Also try different hot sauces.

There is a lot of chips and candy on canteen and that gets old fast. There is also some crackers, but its not too long before you want something else. Colorado DOC serves turkey in place of almost everything. We never get any pork products because some selfish inmates complained about eating pork several years ago. DOC does provide special kosher meals for those who request it, but the inmates still fucked things up for everyone else. So we get turkey-ham and ground turkey for everything. Here at Crowley, they cook the ground turkey in something that makes it taste horrible and it ruins every meal. I think the turkey ham is okay if you take it back and cook it with something to cover its taste. This jerky is pretty good for a microwave turkey jerky.

Turkey-Ham Jerky

Qty.	*Description*	*Commissary #*
2 lb	Turkey-Ham	Kitchen
1/3 cup	Barbeque Sauce	3174
1/8 cup	Honey	3320
1/8 cup	Hot Garlic Chili Sauce	3167
1/8 cup	Picante Hot Sauce	3170
4 pkts	Sugar	3490
4 pkts	Mustard	3800

Approx Cost: $4.50 total

You will also need:
2 Bowls

Cut turkey-ham into strips and microwave 3 minutes. Drain. Combine all other ingredients in a separate bowl to make sauce. Add half of sauce to turkey-ham. Mix well to coat all meat. Microwave 2 minutes. Stir and add half of remaining sauce. Microwave 2 more minutes, stir and add remaining sauce. Mix well and microwave 1-2 more minutes. Meat should be cooked well like jerky but not burnt.

Variations:

Obviously, if you can't get 2 pounds of meat, you can cut the recipe to fit your quantity. You can experiment with different combinations when making the sauce. Try using jelly for a sweeter jerky or use other hot sauces from the gift pack.

"The road to hell is paved with good intentions." Unknown

Chili Cheese Popcorn

Qty.	Description	Commissary #
1 bag	Microwave Popcorn	3185
1 pkt	Chili Ramen Seasoning	3455
2 tbsp	Cheddar Cheese Powder	3165
4 tabs	Butter	Chow

This is as simple as it gets. Pop popcorn in microwave and add butter, seasoning and cheese to bag. (try to distribute evenly) Shake it up and enjoy.

Approx Cost: $1.00 total

The black bean dip in canteen is spicy and a little strange. I like to combine it with refried beans and other stuff. This is a great chip dip.

Cheesy Black Bean Dip

Qty.	Description	Commissary #
5 ea	Beef & Cheese Stick	3018
1/2 bag	Black Bean Dip	3166
1/4 bag	Refried Beans	3005
1/2 cup	Cheddar Cheese Powder	3165
2 tbsp	Dried Onions	3720

Approx Cost: $4.50 total

Set cheese sticks aside.
Chop up the beef sticks as small as possible.
Combine the black beans, refried beans, cheese powder and onions in a bowl. Add just enough hot water to cover beans and mix well.
Microwave 2 minutes and stir it up to break down the dehydrated bean flakes. Add water if it is too thick. (a little goes a long way)
Add the cheese sticks and microwave 1 more minute and stir the cheese into the beans.
You want it to be thick as a chip dip, but not so heavy the chips break. Serve with your favorite chips.

Variations:
You can make it without the beef & cheese sticks if you want to save some cash but it is worth the extra money.

Brewed Iced Tea with Lemon

Qty.	Description	Commissary #
2 tsp	Instant Tea - Nestea	2065
2-3 tsp	Lemonade Mix (optional)	2004

You will also need:
Coffee Maker, 1 Coffee Filter
2-3 sheets of newspaper folded up
Ice, and Sweetener to taste

Approx Cost: $0.25 total

Place coffee filter in coffee maker and put tea and lemonade mix in filter. Put 1/3 pot of water in coffee maker. Fill carafe with ice and place in coffee maker with newspaper between it and the burner. (to prevent heat from melting ice too soon)
Turn coffee maker on and brew iced tea. Turn off immediately when done brewing. Sweeten to taste. Makes 1 coffee pot.

Pop Bottle Hooch

By: Anonymous ;)

Qty.	Description	Commissary #
1 ea	Orange	Chow
35 packets	Real Sugar (1/2 bag)	3490
2 slices	Bread	3010 or Chow

You will also need:
Empty pop bottle (20 oz)
7-10 days cooking time.
Cloth to filter when done.

Approx Cost: $0.60 total

Peel orange and toss peel. Cut up orange and place in empty bottle with all juice. Put sugar and bread in bottle. Fill half way to top with water. (Do not over fill) Cap bottle and wait until it starts building pressure. (about 2 days) Shake bottle and vent off gas about every few hours or as needed. You will be able to smell the alcohol after about 6-7 days. Continue the process until the fermentation is complete. (the hooch is strong enough and most of the sweetness is gone) This takes a total of about 7-10 days depending on the yeast in the bread and the condition of the orange.
Once it is ready, pour it into a tumbler and remove the solids. Filter the liquid through a piece of cloth and enjoy. Makes 1 cup

Remember! Making hooch is a class 2 write-up if you get caught!

Alcatraz Island in San Francisco, CA.
Alcatraz Penitentiary was decommissioned years ago and is a popular tourist attraction. It is one of the few places where free people can explore the inside of a prison.

"I fear neither death nor pain. I fear a cage. To stay behind bars until use and old age accept them. Until valor has lost all chance of recall or desire." *JRR Tolkien - The Two Towers*

Breakfast Meals

Patience:

The first thing most new fish learn in prison is patience. Prison is all about waiting. Waiting for count to clear. Waiting for chow. Waiting for movement, or yard. Waiting to see the case manager. Waiting a week for your canteen. Waiting for a response from the courts. But mostly your entire sentence you'll be waiting for your parole hearing or for your discharge date so you can get back to your real life. For some convicts, your just waiting to die. That's the facts.

I did not have much patience in my real life on the outs, but luckily I learned quickly that its not all about me. Many people never learn though. Those are the ones that scream and holler at the guard to open their cell door every time they return from chow or yard. Think about it... 300 inmates return from yard at the same time and everyone wants in their cell Right Now! One guard is in control of all the doors and can only open one door at a time. Patience guys! The more you throw a fit, the longer you will wait. How would you react if you were the guard and 300 inmates were yelling at you. Not only are you being impatient and discouraging the guard from meeting your needs, you are annoying the rest of the inmates around you forcing them to do your time until one of them has had enough of your tantrum and kicks your ass.

Actually those who have patience say their time goes by very fast and those without are always complaining about all the waiting and how long their sentence is. There is very little you can do to shorten your sentence, and very many things that make your time difficult already. If you learn patience, you might be able to cope in here.

You will be tested during the holidays. Prison depression is no joke and happens to everyone at some point. I "hard time" when I can't be a part of my families life through the holidays especially. They will continue their life without you and you must learn to let go if you are to survive the holidays or if you want to survive prison at all. It is hard for them too, and you must learn patience with all of your relationships, and trust that they are doing fine without you, for now.

"Patience is a virtue that few have learned and many believe to possess." *unknown*

Breakfast Meals

Prison Survival:

When you come to prison, or if you have recently, you will be challenged to fight someone. Here's my last bit of advise. Step up and fight. If you back down or bitch up, your weakness will be known by everyone. You will become somebody's bitch or get your ass kicked until you check in. (request to go to administrative segregation (Ad-Seg) also known as protective custody or P.C.) Some facilities have a pod just for "check-ins" but then everyone knows who the check-ins are. Aggression is high in this environment and most guys resort to fighting to blow off steam. Sex offenders, and weaklings are often the target. If you choose not to fight you will have a hard time in prison. Guys will extort you, charge you rent to avoid an ass kicking every week, and send all their prospects to kick your ass anyways so they can earn their stripes. If you are a piece of shit or have a fucked up case, you might as well check in. If not, don't let them use you as a punching bag, fight back!

Remember, there is no such thing as fair fighting in here. You fight for survival. It seems like everyone watches UFC and wants to be a MMA fighter. But UFC is still sport fighting and has a lot of rules and someone who is skilled in martial arts can still be surprised by someone who has no concern for human life, much less fair fighting. One good chop to his throat or his eyes will usually stop him. Remember you're fighting for survival, not sport. Gang prospects often make the mistake of thinking they can give someone a body shot and be a hero. You will have one chance to earn everyone's respect, and you'd better seriously take it. Don't stop until he's crying like a bitch and toss him into the pod in front of everyone.

Or cry like a bitch yourself and check in. I hear P.C. is nice. Locked down 24/7 for your own protection.

Buena Vista is known for being a gladiator school, there is a lot of violence there, or at least there used to be. Politics are strong and tensions are high.

"The longest distance between any two points is the shortcut."
Chinese Proverb

Twelve Buena Breakfast Burritos

Qty.	*Description*	*Commissary #*
10 scoops	Powdered Eggs	3610
1 tbsp	Dried Onions	3720
4 pks	Salt & Pepper	Chow
2 pk.	Jalapenos (optional)	3350
3 pks	Mozzarella Cheese	3161
1 pk	Bacon (15 slices)	Gift Pack
2 ea	Sausage Hot (or mild)	3345
4-5 ea	Potatoes	Chow
1 bag (12)	Tortillas	3505

You will also need:
12+ pc newspaper wraps
5 Bowls, 1 cup w/ lid
1 Faith items box (if available)

Approx Cost: $16.00 total
Or $1.35 ea

Fill tumbler 3/4 with water. Add egg powder and onions. Mix well. (add 1 tbsp cheese powder to give eggs more realistic color)
Place lid on tumbler and shake egg mixture well, set aside.
Cut up jalapenos, set aside.
Cut up mozzarella cheese, set aside.
Cook bacon in microwave 1 min (until crispy) Set aside.
Cut up sausage and cook in microwave 2 min. Drain fat. Set aside.
Cook potatoes in microwave (if raw), chop up and set aside.
Use bacon grease to coat empty bowl for eggs. Shake eggs again and pour into greased bowl. Cook eggs in microwave 2-3 min stirring every 30 sec. Add salt and pepper and set aside.
Separate tortillas with newspaper and warm in microwave 1 min. Flip and heat 1 more min.
Combine eggs, crumbled bacon, sausage, jalapenos, and potatoes in faith items box or several bowls. Mix well.

Spoon equal amounts of burrito mix onto tortillas. Sprinkle cheese on each one and roll up. Wrap with newspaper. Try adding Hot Sauce to taste. (Tapatio sauce is great on eggs) Or try smothering with Green Chili Sauce. (page 32)
Makes 12 breakfast burritos. Will keep overnight in plastic bag.

Variations:
If you can't get bacon or potatoes, you can use spam or add more eggs. If you can get hamburger patties, real eggs, and/or shredded cheese from the kitchen, you'll be in heaven.

Breakfasts

Two Killer Breakfast Bagels

Qty.	*Description*	*Commissary #*
8 scoops	Powdered Eggs	3610
1 tbsp	Dried Onions	3720
2 pks	Salt & Pepper	Chow
1 pk	Mozzarella Cheese	3161
6 slices	Bacon	Gift Pack
1 ea	Sausage Hot (or mild)	3345
2 ea	Bagels	3275

You will also need:
4 Bowls, 1 cup w/ lid

Approx Cost: $7.00 total
Or $3.50 ea

Fill tumbler 2/3 with water. Add egg powder and onions. Mix well. (add 1 tbsp cheese powder to give eggs more realistic color)
Place lid on tumbler and shake egg mixture well, set aside.
Cut up mozzarella cheese, set aside.
Cook bacon in microwave 30 sec, set aside.
Slice sausage and cook in microwave 2 min. Drain fat. Set aside
Use bacon grease to coat empty bowl for eggs. Shake eggs again.
Place 1/2 of egg mixture in greased bowl and cook eggs in microwave 1-2 min until center is not liquid. (do not stir) Add salt and pepper and set aside. Cook the rest of the eggs the same way so you have 2 cooked egg patties.

Place bottom of bagel in empty bowl. Place half of the sausage on bagel. Place one cooked egg on sausage. Place 3 slices of bacon on egg. Sprinkle half of cheese on bacon. Place top of bagel on cheese and microwave sandwich for 1 min to melt cheese. Repeat process with other bagel. Add hot sauce to taste. Enjoy.
Makes 2 big breakfast sandwiches.

Variations:
Try spam instead of sausage, or squeeze cheese instead of mozzarella. If you can get real eggs and/or shredded cheese from the kitchen, killer!

"We all wear masks. Every one of us must protect our loved ones from the truth of the wickedness of our hearts."

Sarah Conner Chronicles

Two Ordway Omelets

Qty.	*Description*	*Commissary #*
10 scoops	Powdered Eggs	3610
1 tbsp	Dried Onions	3720
2 pks	Salt & Pepper	Chow
2 pk.	Jalapenos (optional)	3350
1 pk	Mozzarella Cheese	3161
1 ea	Spam	3347
8 slices	Bacon	Gift Pack

You will also need:
4 Bowls, 1 cup w/ lid

Approx Cost: $7.50 total
Or $3.75 ea

Fill tumbler 3/4 with water. Add egg powder and onions. Mix well. (add 1 tbsp cheese powder to give eggs more realistic color)
Place lid on tumbler and shake egg mixture well, set aside.
Cut up jalapenos, set aside.
Cut up mozzarella cheese, set aside.
Cut up spam and place in bowl with bacon. Cook in microwave about 1-2 min (until bacon is crispy) Set aside.
Use bacon grease to coat 2 empty bowls for eggs. Shake eggs again. Place 1/2 of egg mixture in each greased bowl and cook eggs in microwave 1 min. Add spam to each omelet and cook 1 more min until center is not liquid. (do not stir) Add salt and pepper then add bacon, jalapenos, and cheese. Cook for 1 more min to melt cheese. Fold eggs over cheese and cook 30 more sec.
Add hot sauce to taste (I recommend Tapatio sauce on eggs)
Makes 2 large omelets.

Variations:
You can substitute sausage for the spam. If you can get potatoes, hamburger patties, real eggs, and/or shredded cheese from the kitchen, do it.

"Always be happy where you are, but never be content to be there." *Kenny Rodgers*

Rifle Huevos Rancheros

Qty.	*Description*	*Commissary #*
10 scoops	Powdered Eggs	3610
1 tbsp	Dried Onions	3720
4 pks	Salt & Pepper	Chow
4 tbsp	Cheddar Cheese Powder.	3165
2 bags	Chili with Beans	3155
4 ea	Tortillas	3505

You will also need:
2 Bowls, 1 cup w/ lid

Approx Cost: $6.50 total
Or $3.25 ea

Fill tumbler 3/4 with water. Add egg powder and onions. Mix well. (add 1 tbsp cheese powder to give eggs more realistic color) Place lid on tumbler and shake egg mixture well, set aside.
Mix cheddar cheese powder in 6-8 tbsp. hot water to a smooth consistency.
Cook chili with beans in microwave 1-2 min until hot, set aside.
Cook eggs in empty bowl in microwave 2-3 min stirring every 30 sec. Add salt and pepper and set aside.
Separate 4 tortillas with newspaper and warm in microwave 30 sec. Flip and heat 30 more sec.

Spoon beans and eggs on the tortillas in equal amounts. Add cheese to each one and wrap like a burrito. Try adding Hot Sauce to taste. Makes 4 huevos rancheros-2 large servings.

Variations:
You can add sausage or bacon. You could also substitute mozzarella cheese or jalapeno squeeze cheese.

"Crawling in my skin, these wounds they will not heal. Fear is how I fall, Confusing what is real." Lincoln Park - Crawling

Lastly, here is some quick and easy breakfasts for those days you are still in a daze or don't feel like cooking.

Bent County Bagel

Approx Cost: $1.30 ea

Qty.	*Description*	*Commissary #*
1 ea	Bagel	3275
1 tub	Butter (optional)	Chow
1 ea	Cream Cheese	3164
2 tbsp	Marion Berry Jam	3325

Separate bagel halves and butter both halves. Toast on coffee maker burner 15-20 min, or hear in microwave 30 sec. Spread cream cheese and jam and enjoy.

Variations:
Peanut butter and honey is good on a bagel too.

Oatmeal Variations

Peanut Butter Oatmeal Approx Cost: $1.00 ea

Qty.	*Description*	*Commissary #*
1/2 cup	Rolled Oats	3328
2 tbsp	Peanut Butter	3340
1 tbsp	Honey (optional)	3320

Cook oats in a bowl with an equal amount of hot water. Add peanut butter and honey. Add sugar to taste.

Choco-Oatmeal Approx Cost: $1.10 ea

Qty.	*Description*	*Commissary #*
1/2 cup	Rolled Oats	3328
1 bag	Plain M&M's	3060

Cook oats in a bowl with an equal amount of hot water. Add M&M's and enjoy.

Vanilla-Apple Oatmeal Approx Cost: $1.30 ea

Qty.	*Description*	*Commissary #*
1/2 cup	Rolled Oats	3328
1 tbsp	Lean Meal (optional)	3600
1 ea	Apple Pie	3390

Combine oats and lean meal and Cook in a bowl with an equal amount of hot water. Add filling from apple pie and enjoy.

Dinner Meals

Masking Injuries:

Once you have been in a scrap, you will likely have noticeable injuries that may be seen by the cops. Most C/O's will pull you over and inquire as to what happened. You can end up in the hole and get a write up for fighting, or worse. The best way to avoid detection is to stay in your cell until the swelling goes down. Don't go to chow or present yourself to the cops by walking around the pod or yard unless you're a snitch and want the attention. Most convicts know how to help you keep hidden for a couple days by bringing you food and keeping tech if necessary.

You may need to go to yard and fake an injury to cover your tracks. Especially if you are expected to show up at work.

Masking injuries is like masking new tattoos. Wear long sleeves and cover your face partially with your beanie and sunglasses. These things should be common sense but you'd be surprised how many new fish don't know what's up.

You learn to be self-reliant in prison. Because you can not get medical attention when you need it, you must take care of most things yourself. Even while you are waiting to see medical. It is common to wait two to three weeks to see a "doctor" after declaring an emergency. Prison medical requires you to be seen by a nurse twice before they will schedule an appointment with the doctor. This is because so many drug addicts come to prison and fake anything to get some drugs. Tylenol is about all we are able to buy on canteen, and the prescriptions at medical are weak, not to mention they do not prescribe any narcotics to inmates. Also, waiting in line every day for one pill is ridiculous.

Before you know it you will be cracking your own back, pulling your own teeth and dressing your own wounds. That's prison.

Dinner Meals

Soups and Stews

I cannot stand ramen noodles, and rarely eat them. When I do, I have to add something to them like beans or cheese and sausage. Everyone has tried nearly everything when it comes to making super soups. In fact many guys in here think the only thing you can cook is soup, and everything else on canteen is simply what you add to your soup.

I hope this cookbook helps you realize there is more to life than ramen noodles. But once in a while it is easy to just eat a damn soup. Or if you are currently in CSP, (Colorado State Penitentiary) or another Maximum Security facility, you have access to very little canteen, or ways to cook, so you'll wind up eating more soups than you can stand.

CSP Ramen Soup Variations

Spicy Cheesy Soup

Qty.	*Description*	*Commissary #*
1 ea	Chili Ramen Noodles	3455
1/3 bag	Refried Beans	3005
1 ea	Jalapeno Squeeze Cheese	3162

Obviously simply combine all ingredients in a bowl with hot water.

Beef On Beef Soup

Qty.	*Description*	*Commissary #*
1 ea	Beef Ramen Noodles	3465
1 ea	Beef Sausage	3343
1 ea	Beef Stew	3480

Cut up sausage and pre-cook in microwave. Cook noodles before adding stew and sausage.

Variations:

You can add anything you want to ramen noodles- fish, chicken, powdered cheese, or even chips. But its still a damn soup.

CSP is the main Super Maximum Security facility in Colorado. There are others, like Centennial, Limon, and Sterling that are or have a Maximum Level but CSP is the Super Max. Locked down 24/7 and only caged yard time with good behavior.

Here is a real soup that takes some time but is worth it.

French Onion Soup

Qty.	*Description*	*Commissary #*
1/3 bag	Dried Onions	3720
6 tabs	Butter	Chow
2 pkts	Beef Ramen Seasoning	3465
4 slices	Bread	3010 or Chow
1/2 tsp	Garlic Powder (optional)	Kitchen
2-3 pkts	Salt & Pepper (optional)	Chow
1 pk	Mozzarella Cheese	3161

Approx Cost: $3.50 total
Or $1.75 ea

You will also need:
Coffee Maker, 2 Bowls

Reconstitute onions in hot water or use 1 cup fresh onion chopped finely. Place 3 tabs butter in coffee pot. Add onions and cook in coffee maker for 45 min to 1 hr until onions are "caramelized" stirring occasionally.
Make beef stock in bowl with 2 beef ramen packets and 4 cups water. Combine with onions in coffee pot. Cook 30-45 min in coffee maker. Add salt & pepper to taste.
Make garlic toast using 4 slices bread, 3 tabs butter and garlic powder. Toast on coffee maker burner until lightly brown on each side. Slice mozzarella cheese thin and set aside
Pour half of soup into empty bowl and place 2 slices toast (cut up as necessary) on top of soup with slices of cheese. Repeat with second bowl and microwave 1-2 min to melt cheese. Enjoy! Makes 2 servings.

Variations:
You can make a vegetable soup in much the same way using all the vegetables you can get, (dehydrated or fresh from the kitchen) and some salt, pepper, and 1/4 cup of flour in your coffee pot. Add chicken ramen seasoning if you like. Cook for a couple hours.

"The world is trouble. A man needs a little madness or else he dare not cut the rope that sets him free." Unknown

This is a great meal in the winter. It really warms you up. When I was a kid, my mom would make stew and call it "poison." ;) I hated it as a kid but I wish I could have some of her "poison" now!!

Beef / Vegetable Stew

Qty.	*Description*	*Commissary #*
1/2 bag	White Rice	3327
5 tbsp	Dried Carrots (1/3 bag)	3700
5 tbsp	Dried Green Beans (1/3 bag)	3710
2 tbsp	Dried Onions (1/8 bag)	3720
4 tbsp	Dried R/G Peppers (1/4 bag)	3730
2 tbsp	Dried Tomatoes (1/8 bag)	3740
4 tbsp	Vegetable Flakes (1/4 jar)	3168
2 bag	Beef Stew	3480
4 pks	Salt & Pepper	Chow
1 sleeve	Saltine Crackers	3295

You will also need:
2 Bowls, 12-18 hours stew time.

Approx Cost: $8.00 total
Or $4.00 ea

Mix all dehydrated vegetables with 1/2 bag rice and soak in full bowl of hot water. Let stand overnight. Strain water into cup. Separate rice / vegetables into 2 bowls, and add 1 bag of beef stew to each bowl. Add strained water back as necessary to a medium consistency. Mix well.
Microwave 1-2 min until hot. Add salt and pepper to taste and serve with saltines.

Variations:
You can substitute Roast Beef with Gravy (#3370) for one of the bags of beef stew for more beef. Combine both and microwave separately from rice, and then mix equal amounts into rice bowls. Try adding chicken, and garlic powder if you can get it.

Sterling is a large facility with a high side, (medium-closed, and max) and a low security side. It has a kill fence all the way around and houses all types of convicts.

Sterling Stew on Rice

Qty.	Description	Commissary #
1 bag	White Rice	3327
1 tbsp	Dried Onions	3720
2 bag	Beef Stew	3480
4 pks	Salt & Pepper	Chow
1 sleeve	Saltine Crackers	3295

You will also need:
2 Bowls

Approx Cost: $4.50 total
Or $2.25 ea

Mix onions and rice. Separate into 2 bowls, and soak in equal amounts of hot water. Let sit for 15 min.
Pour 1 bag of beef stew into each bowl of rice.
Microwave 1-2 min until hot. Add salt and pepper to taste and serve with saltines. Makes 2 servings.
Variations:
You can substitute Roast Beef with Gravy (#3370) for one of the bags of beef stew for more beef. Combine both and microwave separately from rice, and then pour equal amounts over rice.

Dad's Cell-Made Chicken Stew

Qty.	Description	Commissary #
2 ea	Chicken Leg	Chow
2 ea	Baked Potato	Chow
1/2 bag	White Rice	3327
5 tbsp	Dried Carrots (1/3 bag)	3700
5 tbsp	Dried Green Beans (1/3 bag)	3710
2 tbsp	Dried Onions (1/8 bag)	3720
4 tbsp	Dried R/G Peppers (1/4 bag)	3730
4 pks	Salt & Pepper	Chow
1 sleeve	Saltine Crackers	3295

You will also need:
Coffee Maker, 2 Bowls
4 hours stew time.

Approx Cost: $5.50 total
Or $2.75 ea

Brew 4 cups of water. (1/3 pot) Chop up potatoes and place in coffee pot. Pull chicken off of bone, chop up and add to coffee pot. Place all the vegetables and rice in pot and let cook for 4 hours. Add salt and pepper to taste. Serve with saltines.

Double Arch in Arches National Park, near Moab, Utah.
One of the last places I visited with my crew before I went to jail.

"For sin shall not be master over you, for you are not under law, but under grace." ***Romans 6:14***

Dinner Meals

Mexican Dishes

Prison Cash $$:

Its amazing how little money people have in prison, and how much value we place on inexpensive things. Men will start a riot over a single stamp or even a soup. Gambling is illegal in prison but many guys sit at the table all day playing poker with 1 cent chips. Old playing cards are marked and used for chips. The cops know what's up and they usually let it go until they want to get their dick hard. Then they take everyone's chips and the house usually has to cancel all debts so they will start over later. Inmates are excited to make a buck or two. They will do a lot for very little in comparison. You can usually get someone to make a custom greeting card for a buck or two. Nearly everything in prison is bought and sold with stamps and soups, but everything is money in here. You want to buy something? You can either order what the guy wants or come off of what you already have. Soups (ramen noodles) are worth 26 cents and practically everyone eats them because they are the cheapest thing on canteen. Stamps are the easiest form of cash in here, and most people will take stamps, but sometimes they will want food or hygiene products.

If you're interested in making a large purchase, you might need to get outside help. You can have your people put money on his books or order him a gift pack. But be very careful! DOC does monitor who is depositing money on who's books. If they think there is something wrong, they just might confiscate the money. Your people can put money on through Ace or Western Union under someone else's name if necessary, or they can arrange to meet someone on the streets. Whatever you decide, be careful. Sometimes the risk isn't worth it.

"You don't choose the things you believe in, they choose you."
unknown

Disposable What??:

It's a trip cooking in prison with disposable plastic sporks and plastic bowls that's for sure. I never placed so much value on such worthless trash as I do in prison. You can't get common everyday items inside, so you hold on to, and reuse containers of any kind. I would never wash or reuse disposable plastic-ware out there. In here I have a couple flimsy plastic sporks that are over a year old (well worn but clean). Most pigs will take your sporks and containers on a shakedown too, so not only do you keep them, but you learn to keep them hidden (as if they are contraband). Pigs need to justify their position somehow and most, if not all of them are pigs for a reason—They relish in fucking with others and degrading, belittling, and abusing people to make themselves feel good. If you don't have any contraband for them to confiscate every couple weeks when they toss your cell, they can take anything and declare it altered or stolen.

Here in Colorado we are able to make many Mexican dishes with what is on canteen. Most of which go great with a smothering sauce. Try this green chili on anything that needs an extra kick. Another tip; you can use Taco Mix in place of sausage in any of these recipes. It is a Soy product and is very salty but you can strain it and flush most of the salt out of it. One whole bag will replace three sausages. It makes about a pound of ground beef (soy).

Dinners

Green Chili Smothering Sauce

Qty.	*Description*	*Commissary #*
1/2 ea	Sausage Hot (or mild)	3345
1 cup	Salsa from chow	Chow
3 tbsp	Hot Sauce	3170
1/3 cup	Flour	Kitchen

Approx Cost: $1.50 total

Cut up 1/2 sausage into small bits and pre-cook in microwave. Add salsa from chow, hot sauce, and 2 cups water. Cook in microwave until boiling. (2-3 minutes) Add flour slowly while stirring. Add hot sauce and mix well until smooth consistency. Cook 1-2 more minutes stirring every 30 sec until sauce is thick enough.

Makes enough sauce to smother 3-4 servings.

One Dozen El Finito Burritos

Qty.	*Description*	*Commissary #*
1 bag	White Rice	3327
2 tbsp	Dried Onions	3720
2 pk.	Jalapenos (optional)	3350
2 bags	Refried Beans	3005
2 ea	Sausage Hot (or mild)	3345
Or 1 bag	*Taco Mix*	*3365*
2 bag	Chili with Beans	3155
¼ cup	Cheddar Cheese Powder.	3165
1 bag (12)	Tortillas	3505

You will also need:
12+ pc newspaper wraps
3 Bowls, 1 cup

Approx Cost: $14.50 total
Or $1.25 ea

Mix onions and rice, and soak in equal amount of hot water.
Cut up jalapenos, set aside.
Mix refried beans in equal amount of hot water. Cook in microwave 1 to 2 min. Stir well.
Cut up sausage (or cook taco mix) and cook in microwave 2 min. Drain fat. Add chili beans and cook 1 more min.
Combine refried beans and chili bean/sausage. Add in jalapenos, mix well.
Mix cheddar cheese powder in 1 cup hot water to a smooth, thin consistency. (Using about 3/4" deep powder in tumbler and add hot water to 2/3 full) Add cheese to rice, mix well.
Separate tortillas with newspaper and warm in microwave 1 min. Flip and heat 1 more min.

Roll burritos with approx. 3 scoops bean mix and 2 scoops rice mix each. Wrap with newspaper. Will keep 2-3 days in plastic bag. Add hot sauce to taste.

Variations:
You can substitute chicken for the sausage, add crushed Tostitos, or add Beef Stew or Beef Tips. Try chopping up tamales (if you can get them) and substituting for one chili beans. Some people use ramen noodles instead of rice for a somewhat cheaper recipe. Try to get hamburger patties and/or shredded cheese from the kitchen.
Try smothering with Green Chili Sauce.

Two Stadium Style Nachos

Qty.	Description	Commissary #
1 ea	Sausage Hot (or mild)	3345
2 pk.	Jalapenos (optional)	3350
1/3 cup	Cheddar Cheese Powder.	3165
1 pk	Squeeze Cheese	3162
1 bag	Tostitos Chips	3205

You will also need:
3 Bowls, 1 cup

Approx Cost: $6.00 total
Or $3.00 ea

Cut up sausage and cook in microwave 2 min. Drain fat.
Cut up jalapenos, set aside.
Mix cheddar cheese powder in 1-1/2 cups hot water to a smooth, medium-thick consistency. (Using about 1" deep powder in tumbler and add hot water to 3/4 full) Add squeeze cheese.
Place chips in two bowls. Heat in microwave 1 min.
Pour cheese on chips. Add sausage, and jalapenos. Enjoy.

Variations:
Try beef crumbles if you can get them. Try beans and chili spice.

Two Ft. Lyon Frito Pies

Qty.	Description	Commissary #
1 ea	Sausage Hot (or mild)	3345
1 bag	Chili with Beans	3155
2 pk.	Jalapenos (optional)	3350
1/4 cup	Cheddar Cheese Powder.	3165
1 pk	Squeeze Cheese	3162
1/2 bag	Fritos Chips	3175

You will also need:
3 Bowls, 1 cup

Approx Cost: $6.50 total
Or $3.25 ea

Cut up sausage and cook in microwave 2 min. Drain fat. Add chili beans and cook 1 more min. Add cut up jalapenos.
Mix cheddar cheese powder in 1 cup hot water to a smooth, medium-thick consistency. (Using about 3/4" deep powder in tumbler and add hot water to 1/2 full) Add squeeze cheese.
Place Fritos in two bowls. Pour chili mix over Fritos, heat in microwave 1 min. Pour cheese over Fritos / chili. Enjoy.

4 Chili Rellanos

Qty.	*Description*	*Commissary #*
4 large	Anaheim Chili Peppers	Greenhouse
2-3 slices	Dried Bread	3010 or Chow
1/2 bowl	Tostitos Chips (crushed)	3205
5 scoops	Powdered Eggs	3610
1 tbsp	Dried Onions (optional)	3720
2 pk	Mozzarella Cheese	3161

You will also need:
3 Bowls, 1 cup w/ lid

Approx Cost: $6.50 total
Or $1.65 ea

Place chili peppers in bowl and fill with hot water. Microwave 1-2 min to light boil. Set aside.
Crumble dried bread into fine crumbs. Crush Tostitos into fine powder and combine with bread crumbs.
Fill tumbler 1/3 with water. Add egg powder and onions. Mix well. (add 1 tbsp cheese powder to give eggs more realistic color)
Place lid on tumbler and shake egg mixture well, set aside.

Remove chili peppers from hot water after soaking for 5-10 min. Clean peppers by cutting off stem end and gently removing all seeds from inside without splitting sides of peppers. Dry peppers on paper towel or toilet paper.
Cut mozzarella cheese as small as possible and stuff into peppers being careful not to tear peppers.
Combine eggs with bread crumbs and roll chili's in bread mixture. Microwave 2 chili's at a time in a bowl for 2 min to melt cheese. Enjoy! Makes 2 large servings. (2 relanos each)

Add hot sauce or try smothering with Green Chili Sauce. (page 32)

Variations:
If you can't get large peppers you will need to use several small peppers and prepare the breading like a tamale.

"Greater love has no one than this, than to lay down ones life for his friends." John 15:13

Twenty Territorial Tamales

Qty.	*Description*	*Commissary #*
1 bag	Taco Mix	3365
1 bag	Chicken	3515 or Chow
1 bag	Chili with Beans	3155
3 tbsp	Hot Garlic Chili Sauce	3167
1 bag	Tostitos	3205

You will also need:
20+ Plastic wraps, 3 bowls w/ lids

Approx Cost: $9.00 total
Or $0.45 ea

Cook the taco mix in hot water and drain off excess water.
Add the chicken, chili with beans, and hot sauce (or peppers) to the taco mix and cook in microwave 1-2 minutes to make chili filling.
Crush the Tostitos into a fine powder. Separate crumbs into two bowls and add enough hot water to just cover Tostitos and mix well to make a soft dough. Microwave 4-6 min stirring every min. Add water as necessary to maintain a soft dough consistency.
Cut 20 or more plastic wraps 2 inches larger than your bowl lid.
Place a plastic wrap on top side of bowl lid and use the recessed portion of the lid as a mold for your dough. Spoon 1/2 cup of dough onto plastic and spread to fit mold. Place another lid directly on top of dough lining up with the lid underneath and press all around to form your dough to about 1/8" thick making a wrap. Remove excess dough from edges and spoon chili filling into center of dough wrap and roll up with plastic pressing ends together to seal them. Repeat process until all ingredients are used and heat tamales in microwave 1-2 min.
Makes about 20 tamales, or 4 large servings. Will keep overnight.

Variations:
Try substituting roast beef or sausage for taco mix. If you can get fresh jalapenos, or other hot peppers, chop them up and use 4-5 peppers in place of garlic chili sauce.
Try smothering with Green Chili Sauce. (page 32)

Territorial is the oldest prison in Colorado. It began as the only prison for a large territory including Colorado, New Mexico, Wyoming, and Utah, before Colorado was a state. Now Colorado has over 20 prisons. Many of which are larger than Territorial and all are overcrowded.

One Dozen Baja Chicken Burritos

Qty.	*Description*	*Commissary #*
1 bag	White Rice	3327
2 tbsp	Dried Onions	3720
2 pk.	Jalapenos (optional)	3350
1 bag	Refried Beans	3005
1 bag	Black Bean Dip	3166
3 bags	Chicken Chunk, White	3515 or Chow
2 bag	Chili with Beans	3155
1 bag (12)	Tortillas	3505

You will also need:
12+ pc newspaper wraps
3 Bowls, 1 cup

Approx Cost: $18.00 total
Or $1.50 ea

Mix onions and rice, and soak in equal amount of hot water.
Cut up jalapenos, and add to rice.
Mix refried beans with black beans and soak in equal amount of hot water. Cook in microwave 1 to 2 min. Stir well.
Combine chicken and chili beans in bowl and mix well. Cook in microwave 1 to 2 min.
Combine refried beans and chili bean/chicken. Mix well.
Separate tortillas with newspaper and warm in microwave 1 min. Flip and heat 1 more min.

Roll burritos with approx. 3 scoops bean mix and 2 scoops rice mix each. Wrap with newspaper. Will keep 2 days in plastic bag. Add hot sauce to taste.

Variations:
You can add crushed Tostitos, or try chopping up tamales (if you can get them) and substituting for one chili beans. Some people use ramen noodles instead of rice for a somewhat cheaper recipe. Try to get hamburger patties and/or shredded cheese from the kitchen.
Try smothering with Green Chili Sauce. (page 32)

"You either die a hero, or you live long enough to see yourself become a villain." *Batman - The Dark Knight*

Dinners

2 Mexican Pizzas

Qty.	*Description*	*Commissary #*
1 pk	Pizza Kit (Crusts Only)	3360
1 ea	Sausage Hot (or mild)	3345
1/2 bag	Refried Beans	3005
1/4 bag	Taco Mix	3365
2 tbsp	Dried Onions	3720
1 ea	Mozzarella Cheese	3161
2 ea	Jalapenos (optional)	3350 or Greenhse

You will also need:
2 bowls w/ lids

Approx Cost: $7.00 total
Or $3.50 ea

Cut up sausage into small bits and pre-cook in microwave.
Precook crusts in microwave 1 min on heat reflector to make somewhat crispy. Tip: Place heat reflector directly on bottom of microwave. (do not use plastic lid or it will melt)
Combine refried beans, taco mix and onions in bowl and fill with just enough hot water to cover beans. Mix well and cook in microwave 2 min. Add water if needed to get a medium-thick consistency.
Spread bean mixture on pizza crusts. Add sausage crumbles and cheese on top. Add Jalapenos over cheese if you like.
Cook each pizza separately on heat reflector in microwave 1-2 min to melt cheese. Makes 2 servings.

Variations:
Try substituting black beans for the refried beans, and if you can get hamburger patties from the kitchen, crumble a couple up and cook in microwave with a chili soup seasoning packet. Then use the hamburger in lieu of the taco mix.

"Iron helmets will not save - even heroes from the grave. Good men's blood will drain away - while the wicked win the day."
Heinrich Heine - Valkyries

Dinners

Four Crowley Quesadillas

Qty.	*Description*	*Commissary #*
1 ea	Sausage Hot (or mild)	3345
4 tbsp	Cheddar Cheese Powder.	3165
4 ea	Tortillas	3505
4 tabs	Butter	Chow

You will also need:
Coffee Maker, 2 bowls, 1 cup

Approx Cost: $2.75 total
Or $0.70 ea

Cut up sausage into small bits and pre-cook in microwave.
Mix cheddar cheese powder in 6-8 tbsp. hot water to a smooth thick consistency.
Spread 1/4 cheese on center of tortilla making about a 4" circle.
Sprinkle 1/4 sausage on cheese and fold sides of tortilla to center making a hexagon. Butter both sides of quesadilla and cook on coffee maker burner for about 10-15 min per side until lightly toasted. Serve with hot sauce. Makes 2 servings.

Variations:
Try to get some grated cheddar cheese from the kitchen for a perfect quesadilla.

Crowley County Correctional Facility is a private prison in Olney Springs, CO. It is owned and run by C.C.A. but houses only Colorado DOC inmates. It is a Medium-Closed security facility that houses approximately 1700 inmates.

"There's a hole in the world, it's a big black pit and its filled with men who are filled with shit and the vermin of the world all inhabit it... But not for long..." *Sweeny Todd*

Dinner Meals
Italian Dishes

Convict Code:

Convict code is essential for every fish to learn and keep. Those who have no respect learn fast—that this is not *their* home. All of us must share the same space and rarely will anyone get away with disrespect. We are all in green.

Convict code is an unwritten code of conduct that everyone abides by out of respect to keep the peace. At the core of convict code is *respect*. If you do not respect your fellow convicts, you unbalance the scales of peace, and you force other people to do your time. *Do your own time.* Everyone has their problems and everyone has their hustle. Mind your own business and don't bring heat to other convicts. *Respect each other.* We are all in the same shoes. Treat others as you wish to be treated. You have no more rights than anyone else in here. Another big rule is *do not snitch.* "Snitches are bitches and will end up in ditches with stitches." Its us against the cops, period. You are either a convict or a rat. We are already in prison, we don't need more trouble. What goes around, comes around.

Keep yourself and your area clean. Clean up after yourself, your mother doesn't live here. This is another respect issue. We all share the same space and disease is rampant in prison. Staff infections, Hepatitis, MRSA, and many others are very common in prison.
Get what you can from the man, but *don't screw your brother.* Remember that prison services are maintained by us inmates. If you can get away with theft or poor work habits, that's on you. But if you're affecting other inmates' time due to your failure to work, you're only screwing your brothers. This is especially important if you are a porter either in the chow hall or in the pod. If you would rather not work, don't get a job in a position where you are responsible for sanitation. If you are assigned to clean the showers, don't think your getting over on the man when you don't work... You are only screwing your brothers. The cops don't care if the showers are clean, we have to use those showers every day so do your job!

The lasagna on our canteen is okay right out of the bag but lacks cheese. Here is a good recipe for a cheesy lasagna casserole.

Limon Lasagna Casserole

Qty.	*Description*	*Commissary #*
2 pks	Fast Mac (noodles only)	3500
1/4 bag	Taco Mix	3365
20 slices	Pepperoni	3363
2 pks	Lasagna	3355
2 ea	Pizza Kit Sauce Packs (1 kit)	3360
3 pks	Cream Cheese	3164
1 pk	Mozzarella Cheese	3161

You will also need:
3 bowls

Approx Cost: $13.50 total
Or $6.75 ea

Place noodles from 2 packs of fast-mac into a bowl with 3 cups hot water. Let stand 10 min. (save cheese powder for another recipe)
Place 1/4 bag of taco mix in another bowl and flood with hot water. Strain water off immediately to remove salt from taco mix. Add more hot water and strain again. Add 1/2 cup water and mix well. Let stand for a couple min until taco mix has absorbed all the water. Drain excess water if any.
Chop up 20 slices pepperoni very small and add to taco mix
Add lasagna packs and pizza sauce packs to the taco mix.
Drain macaroni completely and add to mix and cook in microwave 1-2 min stirring every 30 sec.
Cut up one mozzarella cheese as small as possible, divide into 2 equal parts. Combine cream cheese with half of mozzarella cheese and mix well. Divide lasagna into 2 bowls and spoon cream cheese into lasagna in separate chunks and sprinkle top with mozzarella cheese. Heat 2 more min in microwave without stirring to melt cheese.
Makes 2 large servings.

Variations:
Try substituting roast beef or sausage for taco mix.

San Carlos is Colorado's psych ward prison. Territorial houses some medically dependant inmates, but San Carlos houses all mentally ill inmates. This spaghetti recipe is not really spaghetti due to the ramen noodles. But I bet if you were in San Carlos, it would taste great.

Two Personal Pepperoni Pizzas

Qty.	*Description*	*Commissary #*
2 pk	Mozzarella Cheese	3161
1 pk	Pizza Kit	3360
1 pk.	Pepperoni	3363

You will also need:
2 Bowls or lids to eat off of

Approx Cost: $8.25 total
Or $4.15 ea

Cut up one mozzarella cheese as small as possible, set aside.
Pizza kit comes with 1 cardboard heat reflector, 2 pizza crusts, and 2 pks of pizza sauce. Place one pizza crust on heat reflector, and place some cheese around edge of pizza to contain sauce. Spread pizza sauce on crust, and sprinkle remaining cheese from 1 whole stick on sauce and add half of pepperoni. Cook in microwave for about 2 min. until cheese is melted. Tip: Place heat reflector directly on bottom of microwave. (do not use plastic lid or it will melt)
Repeat process for second pizza.

San Carlos Spaghetti

Qty.	*Description*	*Commissary #*
2 ea	Ramen Noodles	3455
1 ea	Sausage Hot (or mild)	3345
2 ea	Pizza Kit Sauce Packs (1 kit)	3360
1 pk	Mozzarella Cheese	3161

You will also need:
2 Bowls

Approx Cost: $6.00 total
Or $3.00 ea

Cook ramen noodles in hot water until tender. (do not use seasoning) Drain water off.
Cut up sausage and cook in microwave 2 min. Drain fat. Add both pizza sauce packs and cook 1 more min. (Use pizza crusts in another meal like Mexican Pizza on page 28)
Cut up mozzarella cheese as small as possible and set aside.
Separate noodles into 2 empty bowls, add sauce and sprinkle cheese on top. Makes 2 servings
Variations:
If you can get spaghetti sauce from the kitchen it will taste more like spaghetti and less like pizza.

Dinners

My dog Moe.
I took this picture on my last morning of freedom.

"The strongest memory is weaker than the palest ink."
Chinese Proverb

Dinner Meals

Fish Dishes

Inmate Rights:

That's right, inmates still have rights. You may think you don't have any rights and believe me you don't have much, but we all are protected by the AR's (Administrative Rules), and it would benefit you to learn a little about AR's.

AR's are established by DOC and apply to all inmates. I cannot possibly list all the AR's here as the book is several hundred pages, but you can access them in the law library, through your case manager, or your people can research them online for you. Many of them restrict what we as inmates are allowed to do, but some of them protect us from the officers as well. Things like how many hot meals per day they are required to provide, and how long they can lock us down without a shower or even how many microwaves they must provide in the pod. The facilities are always trying to push the boundaries of what they are required to provide in order to control costs and feed their desire to treat inmates like animals. It is unfortunate, but true. So get to know the AR's and file grievances whenever you need the facility to correct something.

You can get grievance forms from your case manager, and usually you would file your grievance with the case manager. There are multiple steps to the process and you must keep on them to get a response, but you will. As long as you are professional in the way you handle your grievance with them, and your issue is legitimate, you will get positive results.

POR's are simply Posted Operational Rules the unit staff or facility makes up that are specific to that unit or area of the facility. Sometimes the POR's are in conflict with the AR's so if you are familiar with the AR's and have a problem with one of their POR's, you can challenge them on it. But be careful, if you poke the bear too often he will bite you.

Cops have a way of making your time difficult and love to do it so don't give them a reason to if you don't have to.

Prison Politics:

Prison politics can be tough to grasp at first but its just as important as convict code. One thing is for sure, we are all in prison, but you will either be a convict, or an inmate. It depends on your attitude. Most guys that have been down a long time are convicts. They follow the convict code and expect everyone else to do the same. They come from a time where riots were a common occurrence, and if you disrespected someone you got stuck. They also keep a strong separation between themselves and cops.

There is a new breed of inmate currently entering the system. Many new inmates are soft. Either they are youngsters and have little respect, or they are pushovers and just don't care to stick to a convicts way of life. Soft inmates are generally new fish but old timers can be passive inmates as well.

We are all in the same boat, unless you are a leg-rider, a rat or a snitch—then you must be dealt with. Pieces of shit (undercover cops, rats, and disrespectful inmates) are targeted and usually forced to check-in or get fucked up and end up in the hole or Ad-Seg anyway.

The most hated or targeted of all inmates are sex offenders. Nobody cares to associate with a sick child molester, so many convicts will want to see your paperwork before they associate with you. Sex offenders are usually forced to check-in as well, so many try to keep hidden.

I personally (unlike most convicts) don't care what your in for. I will judge your character in here, which is more relevant anyhow.

Gangs are a huge part of prison as many *real* gangs help to clean up their own backyard (police their own), and demand respect from other gang members. In reality, many new fish are scared shitless when they arrive and feel they need to click-up for their own protection. Thus many gangs are made up of scared individuals who don't truly respect other gangs and feel a false sense of security together. That's where some riots evolve. (Besides genuine gang rivalry.) Not to mention the fact that a gang of weaklings is not a gang.

Most prisons were segregated years ago. Blacks, whites, Hispanics, and rival gangs were not allowed to live together. Now we are forced to live together. Older convicts are used to the segregation and therefore are not very tolerant of other races. The chow hall used to be segregated as well, where blacks sat at certain tables and white supremacists at the other end of the chow hall. Convicts will still only sit with their own. It is best to stick with your own people and mind your own business.

Six Monterrey Fish Burritos

Qty.	*Description*	*Commissary #*
1 bag	White Rice	3327
2 tbsp	Dried Onions	3720
2 tbsp	Dried R/G Peppers (1/8 bag)	3730
1 pkt	Chili Ramen Seasoning	3455
1 tbsp	Garlic Powder	Kitchen
1 bag	Salmon	3513
Or 2 bags	*Tilapia*	*3520*
12 pkts	Mayonnaise	3803
4 scoops	Powdered Eggs	3610
1/2 bag (6)	Tortillas	3505
1 sleeve	Snack Crackers (Ritz)	3290

You will also need:
6+ pc newspaper wraps
2 Bowls, 1 cup

Approx Cost: $6.50 total
Or $1.10 ea

Mix 1 tbsp onions, 2 tbsp peppers, chili ramen packet, and garlic powder with rice, and soak in equal amount of hot water.
In another bowl, combine 1 tbsp onions and 3 packets mayonnaise with salmon or tilapia and stir well.
Fill tumbler 1/8 with water. Add powdered eggs and mix well. Pour over fish and microwave 1-2 min until eggs are cooked.
Combine fish mixture with rice. Add 9 more packets mayonnaise. Mix well.
Wrap burritos with equal amounts to make 6 burritos. Crush snack crackers over salmon mix before rolling up burritos.

Variations:
You can add ranch dressing or use hot sauce if you like.

"Time passes. Even when it seems impossible. Even when each tick of the second hand aches like the pulse of blood behind a bruise. It passes unevenly, in strange lurches and dragging lulls but pass it does, even for me."

Stephenie Meyer - New Moon

This was a nice surprise when trying to create a sweet and sour fish dish. Tilapia is one of my favorite fishes because it is not as fishy or salty. (I can't stand Mackerel) Commissary just added Tilapia to the canteen so I'm excited to add a good fish dish. Enjoy!

Sweet/Hot Tilapia on Rice

Qty.	*Description*	*Commissary #*
Rice:		
1 bag	White Rice	3327
2 tbsp	Dried Onions	3720
2 tbsp	Dried R/G Peppers (1/8 bag)	3730
2 tbsp	Dried Carrots (1/8 bag)	3700
1 tbsp	Garlic Powder	Kitchen
Sauce:		
5 pkts	Sugar	3490
4 pkts	Ketchup	3801
1 tbsp	Garlic Chili Sauce	3161
2 pkts	Soy Sauce	3172
3 pkts	Mustard	3800
2 tbsp	Honey	3320
2 tbsp	White Vinegar	Kitchen
or 2 pks	*Jalapenos*	*3350*
2 bags	Tilapia	3520
5 scoops	Powdered Eggs	3610

You will also need:
3 Bowls, 1 tumbler w/ lid

Approx Cost: $8.50 total
Or $4.25 ea

Combine all dried vegetables and garlic powder with rice and add an equal amount of hot water. Cover and let stand.
In another bowl, make sauce by combining the remaining ingredients except the fish and jalapenos. If you can't get vinegar, use 2 pkts jalapenos for the juice, by squeezing all the juice out of them as you can. You can use one of the jalapenos (chopped finely) in the sauce as well. Mix sauce and add 2-3 tbsp water if necessary to get a thin consistency. Add Tilapia and all lemon juice into the sauce and cook in microwave 2-3 min stirring every 30 sec until thickened.
Fill tumbler 1/3 with water. Add egg powder and mix well. Place lid on tumbler and shake egg mixture well. Pour into bowl and cook in microwave 2 minutes stirring every 30 sec. Add scrambled eggs to rice and mix well. Pour fish / sauce over rice.
Makes 2 servings.

Mackerel Over Noodles

Qty.	*Description*	*Commissary #*
Noodles:		
1 bag	Rice Noodles	Gift Pack
2 tbsp	Dried Onions	3720
Sauce:		
5 pkts	Sugar	3490
1 tbsp	Garlic Powder	Kitchen
6 pkts	Ketchup	3801
2 tbsp	Garlic Chili Sauce	3161
6 pkts	Soy Sauce	3172
6 pkts	Mustard	3800
3 tbsp	Honey or Jelly	3320
2 bag	Mackerel Fillets	3385

Approx Cost: $5.50 total
Or $2.75 ea

You will also need:
3 Bowls

Combine dried onions with rice noodles and add an equal amount of hot water. Cover and let stand.
In another bowl, make sauce by combining the remaining ingredients except the fish. You can use one pack of jalapenos (chopped finely) in the sauce as well. Mix sauce and add 2-3 tbsp water if necessary to get a thin consistency.
Clean mackerel removing all the bones you can. Add mackerel into the sauce and cook in microwave 2-3 min stirring every 30 sec until thickened.
Cook noodles in microwave if necessary to speed up process. Drain off all water and separate noodles into 2 bowls.
Pour fish / sauce over noodles.
Makes 2 servings.

Variations:
You can add hot sauce or barbeque sauce to the sauce if you like.
You can use regular ramen noodles instead of the rice noodles.

"Redemption is a funny thing - sometimes you have to go through hell to get it." *Unknown*

Dinners

Tuna Casserole

Qty.	*Description*	*Commissary #*
2 ea	Chicken Cup-O-Noodles	3460
2 ea	Fast Mac&Cheese	3500
1 ea	Ramen Noodles	3465
2 pks	Tuna	3510
¼ cup	Cheddar Cheese Powder	3165

You will also need:
2 Bowls

Approx Cost: $6.00 total
Or $3.00 ea

Crush up ramen noodles and place 1/2 in each bowl. (Do not use seasoning packet.) Add 1 Cup-O-Noodles and 1 Fast-Mac to each bowl. Mix in enough hot water to cover noodles.
Add 1/8 cup cheese powder and mix well. Let stand 5 min.
Add 1 pack of tuna to each bowl.
Microwave for 1-2 minutes until noodles are done.
Try adding Hot Sauce to taste. Makes 2 large bowls.

Variations:
You can substitute Rice Noodles from Gift Pack for ramen noodles and Cup-O-Noodles.

Tuna Egg Sandwiches

Qty.	*Description*	*Commissary #*
4 scoops	Powdered Eggs	3610
2 tbsp	Dried Onions	3720
1 pk	Tuna	3510
6 pkt	Mayonnaise	3803
4 slices	Bread	3010

You will also need:
2 Bowls, 1 cup w/ lid

Approx Cost: $3.00 total
Or $1.50 ea

Fill tumbler 1/4 with water. Add egg powder and onions. Mix well. (add 1 tbsp cheese powder to give eggs more realistic color) Place lid on tumbler and shake egg mixture well. Pour egg mixture in bowl and microwave 1-2 min stirring every 30 sec.
Combine tuna and mayonnaise in another bowl and mix well. Gently add in eggs, and spoon onto bread. Makes 2 sandwiches.

Our Criminal Justice System:

I know, everyone thinks convicted felons are the worst of society, and all felons claim the "system" doesn't work or they were screwed. I was once out there and thought poorly of felons too. I never thought I would go to prison. I was a productive member of society and had a strong desire to abide by our laws. But I screwed up and broke the law. However, I am in here because I chose to confess my crime and take responsibility for my actions. I was eligible for probation, and hoped my cooperation might be considered, when I was sentenced to prison. I did believe I got screwed for a short while, but I now feel this is the best place for me… for now. In my time here, I have learned a lot about our "system," through my case as well as many other cases and have a unique perspective.

Believe it or not, our country depends on incarcerations for much of its economic or financial stability. Prisoners are truly a cash crop. The government charges taxpayers thousands of dollars per inmate, and the more convictions they have, the more money they get. Whenever the government is short funds and wants to raise taxes, they threaten to release inmates until the people agree to pay more taxes. And they continue to sentence thousands of new people every year to ridiculous prison terms, completely overcrowding the whole prison system. Currently the United States holds more prisoners than nearly the rest of the world combined. Our criminal justice system is corrupt and ruthless. (like most of our government agencies) The police are required to break nearly every law in the act of enforcing the law. They are above the law and take every advantage because nobody will challenge them. The American People are infatuated with police brutality and illegal tactics. Watch any TV lately? Nearly 80 percent of the shows currently on TV are cop shows. Why? Because that's what people want to watch. Its entertaining to watch cops hunt their prey with blatant disregard for human rights. We all love how they force their suspects into a confession or into snitching on someone else using strong-arm tactics and coercion. They hold you or your loved ones prisoner and perform illegal searches and violate your rights and privacy in the name of justice. They act more like the mob than respectful public servants. It is fun to watch until you are the "suspect," then you'll know the reality of it. It can and will happen to you or someone close to you in your lifetime. That is a fact. The odds are stacked against you so be careful.

Dinner Meals
Other Dishes

Presumed Innocent?:

It's true, many people belong in prison for what they've done, or what they will do if released. But not everyone in prison belongs in prison. In fact most of us in here are just like you. You can be accused of something and suddenly its your responsibility to prove the accusations wrong. Whatever happened to "innocent until proven guilty?" Yeah right… we *all* know better than that.

You might be fingered by someone by mistake or by someone who has it in for you, and you'll be charged with a crime based solely on a snitch's word. Then the detectives and DA's will press so many ridiculous charges that your head will spin. Or they will hold your family hostage, or threaten to add more charges or give you the maximum sentence if you don't take the plea deal.

Next thing you know, your pleading guilty to something under duress or coercion. Possibly something you never did. Even if you were guilty to some extent, they will try to make it unacceptable to you to take your chances in trial.

Then if you don't take a plea deal, you can get convicted on hear-say and circumstantial evidence in trial. Happens <u>every day.</u> Then judges hand out years in prison like they're handing out candy! You could get 20 years or even Life for something that was all a big misunderstanding. That's America for ya. The land of the snitch and the home of the slave!

I'm the last person I ever thought would go to prison. All of my family and friends will agree with that. If it can happen to me, it can happen to you. Stay away from trouble, and if you get into trouble, do not cooperate with the cops, because it will only land you in prison. Get a good attorney and stick to your guns. Remain silent. Don't waive any hearings, or any rights. Don't plead guilty to anything. Make them work for your conviction. Cooperation is seen as a sign of guilt and exploited by every DA, every day.

"No, make no mistake, its not revenge he's after… It's a reckoning." ***Doc Holliday - Toumbstone***

This is a very common meal in here. You would be hard pressed to find someone who doesn't know what a fat bastard is.

Two Four Mile Fat Bastards

Qty.	*Description*	*Commissary #*
1 pk	Mozzarella Cheese	3161
1 ea	Sausage Hot (or mild)	3345
1 pk.	Jalapenos (optional)	3350
2 ea	Bagels	3275

You will also need:
2 Bowls

Approx Cost: $4.00 total
Or $2.00 ea

Cut up mozzarella cheese, set aside.
Slice sausage and cook in microwave 2 min. Drain fat. Set aside
Cut up jalapenos, set aside.
Place bottom of bagel in empty bowl. Place half of the sausage on bagel. Place half of jalapenos on each sandwich. Place half of cheese sausage/jalapenos. Place top of bagel on cheese and microwave each sandwich for 1-2 min to melt cheese. Enjoy.
Makes 2 bagel sandwiches.

Variations:
You can add chili with beans for a sloppy fat bastard.

Four Mile is a MR (Minimum-Restricted) facility in the Cañon City Complex. It is just like Arrowhead.

"An elected legislature can trample a man's rights just as easily as a king can." *The Patriot*

Sweet and Sour Chicken

Qty.	*Description*	*Commissary #*
Rice:		
3/4 bag	White Rice	3327
5 scoops	Powdered Eggs	3610
3 tabs	Butter	Chow
Sauce:		
8 pkts	Sugar	3490
3 tbsp	White Vinegar	Kitchen
or 2 pks	*Jalapenos*	*3350*
3 pkts	Ketchup	3801
1/2 tbsp	Garlic Chili Sauce	3161
2 pkts	Soy Sauce	3172
4 pkts	Mustard	3800
2 tbsp	Honey or Jelly	3320
2 bags	Chicken	3515 or Chow
1/2 cup	Chopped Fresh Bell Peppers	Kitchen
1 pack	Chopped Peanuts (3 oz)	3050

You will also need:
3 Bowls, 1 tumbler w/ lid

Approx Cost: $10.00 total
Or $5.00 ea

Cook rice in equal amount of hot water until mildly soft - Not overcooked. Drain excess water.
Fill tumbler 1/3 with water. Add egg powder and mix well. Place lid on tumbler and shake egg mixture well. Pour into bowl and cook in microwave 2 minutes stirring every 30 sec. Add scrambled eggs and butter to rice and mix well. Cook in microwave 1-2 min stirring every 30 sec.
In another bowl, make sauce by combining the remaining ingredients except the chicken and peppers. If you can't get vinegar, use 2 packets jalapenos for the juice, by squeezing all the juice out of them as you can. You can use one of the jalapenos (chopped finely) in the sauce as well. Add chicken into the sauce and cook in microwave 2 min stirring every 30 sec. Add chopped peppers and chopped peanuts and cook 1-2 more min.
Pour chicken / sauce over rice.
Makes 2 servings.

Variations:
You can try adding hot sauce and getting sesame seeds for Sesame Chicken.

Barbeque Chicken Sandwiches

Qty.	Description	Commissary #
4 slices	Bread	3010
2 tubs	Butter	Chow
1 bag	Chicken	3515
4 tbsp	Barbeque Sauce	3174
1 tbsp	Honey	3320
1 pkg	Mozzarella Cheese	3161

Approx Cost: 7.20 total
Or $3.60 ea

You will also need:
1 Bowl, coffee maker

Toast bread by lightly buttering both sides and placing on coffee maker burner for 15 minutes until golden brown. Flip and toast opposite side, then repeat with the rest of the slices. (toasting is optional as it is time consuming and you may not have a coffee maker, but it is worth it if you do)
Slice mozzarella cheese thinly and place on toast while toasting second side to melt cheese. Repeat with all four slices.
Combine chicken, barbeque sauce and honey in a bowl and cook in microwave 2 minutes. Mix well.
Spoon half of chicken mixture onto bread and make 2 sandwiches.

Variations:
You can bring back your chow hall chicken (a couple pieces will do) just be careful to remove all the bones.

Combination Fajitas

Qty.	*Description*	*Commissary #*
2 bags	Roast Beef and Gravy	3370
2 bags	Chicken	3515
4 pkts	Italian Dressing	Chow
4 pkts	Soy Sauce	3172
2 pkts	Ketchup	3801
1 whole	Onion	Kitchen
or 1/4 bag	Dehydrated Onions	3720
1 whole	Bell Pepper	Kitchen
1 whole	Tomato	Kitchen
6 tubs	Butter	Chow
1/2 bag (6)	Tortillas	3505

You will also need:
3 Bowls, 8-12 hours marinade time.

Approx Cost: $14.00 total
Or $7.00 ea

Remove most of the gravy from the roast beef by placing in bowl and rinsing with water. Pat dry and add chicken.
In another bowl, combine the Italian dressing, soy sauce, and ketchup. Mix well and add the roast beef and chicken to the sauce. Put a lid on the bowl of meat and let marinade for 8-12 hours

When you are ready to cook, clean and chop onion, bell pepper, and tomato. Set aside. If you are using any dehydrated vegetables, reconstitute them now by placing them in hot water for 30 minutes.
In two clean bowls, heat 3 tubs butter each in microwave until melted and hot about 30-45 sec. Add half of onions and bell peppers to each bowl and cook 1-2 minutes. Add half of the meat mixture to each bowl and cook 2-3 min stirring every 20 sec.
Warm 6 tortillas in microwave on newspaper 45 sec.
Serve with chopped tomatoes. Makes two servings.

Variations:
Add hot sauce or other peppers. You can use chicken from chow and substitute it for all the meat if you get 4-5 pieces.

"I have long feared that my sins will return to visit me... and the cost is more than I can bear." *The Patriot*

My sister - Tara took this picture.
I like to think it represents our path or our future. Sure is peaceful.

"Don't steal tomorrow from God's hands. Give Him time to speak and reveal His will. He is never late - learn to wait."

LB Cowman -Streams In The Desert

Desserts

Got Religion?:

A common expectation among many people inside and outside prison is that convicted felons "find God" in prison. It also seems to be generally accepted that those prisoners who become religious in prison are phony hypocrites. They either just want to hide their sins or they are trying to manipulate others with their new faith. Maybe some of them are. But not all converted convicts are phony.

Unfortunately, God is not a subject most people are comfortable talking about. I think people who have a real belief or even a relationship with their lord keep that personal in an attempt to not appear foolish to those who do not have faith. Those who do not have religion, tend to look down on religious people, as if they are mindless followers.

At the risk of looking like a fool, I am going to tell you my story. I was one of the non-believers for most of my life. I am ashamed to admit that I did look down on people of faith. I married a Christian 19 years ago and we lived in a house divided. She went to church and I went to work. I was not an atheist, I did believe there must be a God, I just had no use for Him. I believed the churches were brainwashing people and lying to people, and I had no interest in joining their "cult." I was even upset when my own kids would come home from church with WWJD paraphernalia. I was stressed and depressed and eventually became suicidal. I started taking extreme risks in my life and doing things I never thought I could do because of my depression and actually believed that if I finally got caught, I could kill myself to escape whatever consequences.

I was at the breaking point and the heat was on when I last attempted suicide. That's when my life changed. I wasn't looking for God but He found me. As I stood over a cliff early in the morning on Lookout Mountain, I was finally about to jump when the sun peeked over the horizon. I had to stop and admire the beauty. I always loved sunsets and I loved to look at the city lights of Denver from Lookout Mountain at night. But I never watched the sunrise over the city lights. It overwhelmed me with beauty. I then felt a warmth deep inside like I've never felt. Suddenly I was filled with love and peace. I could not remember why I was about to jump. I stood there for a few minutes and I suddenly knew what I had to do. It was like someone or something placed a whole new understanding in my heart. I had experienced the love of Jesus and I knew then that He does exist and He is going to fix me. I confessed my crimes that day and began to live for Him. I'm in prison now for what I did, but I am at peace.

I suppose it happens to everyone at some point. Some of us are just so hard headed that God needs us on our knees to get our attention.

This is a top seller in the pods. Especially around Christmas time. You can sell these for 5 stamps all day long and make almost a buck a piece. Another hot item is suckers. People melt taffy to make suckers but it over works the microwaves and they quit working rather quickly. So it causes a lot of friction in the pod when you break a microwave. Sometimes it takes months for the cops to replace it.

Freemont Fudge Bars

Qty.	*Description*	*Commissary #*
2 ea	Graham Crackers	3280
3 tabs	Butter	Chow
or 2 tbsp	Honey	3320
1/2 cup	Hot Cocoa Powder	2015
3 tbsp	Creamy Peanut Butter	3340

You will also need:
1 Bowl, 1 microwave meal tray

Approx Cost: $1.30/bar

Crush graham crackers finely and add butter or honey. Mix well and press into bottom of a plastic tray from any microwave meal, or use whatever you can to make a bar about 3” by 5”

In bowl, mix cocoa with 6 tbsp water. Microwave 1 min or until cocoa foams up to top of bowl. Stir well and cook 30 more sec. Stir again and cook 30 more sec. Add peanut butter and mix well. Pour over crust in tray. Let cool 4-6 hours. Makes 1 fudge bar.

Tip: You can measure cocoa and water with a scoop from powdered eggs. Use 8 scoops cocoa and 4 scoops water for a more accurate mix. Experiment with the quantities to get the consistency you like.

Variations:
You certainly don't need a crust, and you can add M&M’s or granola, or nuts to the mix. If you don't care for a “peanut butter fudge,” try my German Chocolate Granola Bars on page 62.

"I found a reason for me... To change who I used to be. A reason to start over new. And the reason is you."

Hoobestank - Reason

This is one of my favorites! It is just like real cheesecake on the outs.

Cañon City Cherry Cheesecake

Qty.	*Description*	*Commissary #*
1 sleeve	Graham Crackers	3280
35 pkts	Sugar	3490
16 tabs	Butter	Chow
10 ea	Cream Cheese Packs	3164
1 scoop	Powdered Eggs	3610
4 ea	Cherry Pies	3395

You will also need:
2 Bowls, 1 cup

Approx Cost: $11.50 total

Crush graham crackers into fine crumbs. Add 15 sugar packets, mix well. Melt 16 tabs of butter (8 tbsp) in microwave and add to graham cracker crumbs. Mix well and press into sides and bottom to form crust about 1/4 inch thick and about half way up the side.
In cup, mix 1 scoop of egg powder with 2-3 tbsp water. (or use 1 egg from the kitchen)
In separate bowl, combine all cream cheese, remaining sugar packets (20 pkts) and egg mix. Microwave 1-2 min stirring every 30 sec until smooth. Pour into crust right away.
Chill on ice for 4 hours.
Remove cherry filling from 4 cherry pies and place on top of cheesecake once pie has set. Makes one pie - 4 servings.

Variations:
You can melt a Nestle chocolate bar and pour on crust before adding cream cheese for a chocolaty crust. If you can't get the butter, you can substitute honey, it actually works well but is considerably more expensive.

"I'm not crazy, I'm just a little impaired. I know right now you don't care, but soon enough you're gonna think of me, and how I used to be" *Matchbox 20 - Unwell*

German Chocolate Granola Bars

Qty.	*Description*	*Commissary #*
1/2 cup	Rolled Oats (Dry)	3328
1/2 jar	Peanut Butter	3335
25 pkts	Sugar	3490
1/2 cup	Hot Cocoa Powder	2015
4 ea	Nestle Crunch Bars	3020
1 box	German Chocolate Cookie Rings	3400
1/3 bag	Low Fat Cereal (Granola)	3250
3 tbsp	Lean Meal	3600

You will also need:
2 Bowls, 1 plastic bag

Approx Cost: $9.50 total

Grind oats into a powder as much as possible. Combine peanut butter and oats in a bowl. Add sugar and cocoa and 3-4 tbsp water. Mix well and cook in microwave 1-2 min stirring every 30 sec until soft and well mixed.
Break up Nestle Crunch bars and German Chocolate Cookie Rings in another bowl. Add cereal and lean meal and mix well. Melt in microwave 1-2 min stirring every 30 sec.
Combine peanut butter and chocolate from both bowls and heat in microwave another 1-2 min stirring every 30 sec. Let cool 10 minutes, and pour contents into a clean, empty tortilla bag or similar bag. You can then spread the chocolate like dough into a slab about 3/4" thick.
Let cool in bag 2-3 hours and cut into bars.

Variations:
You can layer the chocolate and peanut butter in a bowl and let it cool 2-3 hours and then cut it like a pie. You can also experiment with other candy bars and whatever you like. I use lean meal for the vanilla flavor, or you can use vanilla creamer if you have it.

"What lies behind us and what lies ahead of us are tiny matters compared to what lies within us."

Emerson

Duplex Cookie Cake

Qty.	*Description*	*Commissary #*
4 pks	Duplex Sandwich Cookies	3220
2 tbsp	Vanilla Creamer	Gift Pack
1 ea	Wild Cherry Pepsi	Vending Machine
1/4 cup	Milk	2060 or Chow

You will also need:
2 Bowls, 1 cup

Approx Cost: $4.50 total

Separate all of the duplex cookies (like Oreo's) and scrape all the creamy centers into a bowl for use on icing later.
Crush all cookies into a powder in another bowl. Add creamer and mix well. Pour 6-8 oz Wild Cherry Pepsi into cookie crumbs one ounce at a time while mixing to make the crumbs into a dough. (Do not use too much Pepsi or it will be too soft)
Bake cake in microwave 3-4 min without stirring until dough is firm in the center but not burnt on the edges. (Check often while baking)
Make icing with cookie centers and milk adding a small amount of milk at a time while stirring until icing is the right consistency. You can add cocoa or creamer for flavoring if you like.
Allow cake to cool in bowl at least 1 hour and frost with your icing right in the bowl. Cut like a pie and enjoy!

Variations:
You can crush chocolate chip cookies into the mix or add M&M's.
You can use any soda pop but Wild Cherry Pepsi tastes best.

"We all have weak moments. Moments when we lose our faith. But its our flaws, our weaknesses, that make us human."
Sarah Conner Chronicles

Orange Chocolate Bars

Qty.	*Description*	*Commissary #*
1/2 cup	Hot Cocoa Powder	2015
1/4 cup	Tang	2050
4 ea	Hershey Almond	2035

You will also need: Approx Cost: $4.30 total
1 Bowl, 1 plastic bag (tortilla bag)

In a bowl, mix cocoa with 6 tbsp water. Microwave 1 min or until cocoa foams up to top of bowl. Stir well and cook 30 more sec. Stir again and cook 30 more sec. Add tang and mix well.
Crush Hershey bars into cocoa and melt in microwave 1-2 min.
Pour into plastic bag and spread out to 1/4" thick. Let cool 4-6 hours. Cut into pieces and enjoy.

Variations:
You can add M&M's or granola, or nuts to the mix.

Nutty Bar Cheesecake

Qty.	*Description*	*Commissary #*
1 box	Nutty Bars	3425
1/2 jar	Peanut Butter	3340
8 pks	Cream Cheese	3164
20 pks	Sugar	3490

You will also need: Approx Cost: $8.50 total
2 Bowls

Crush all nutty bars in a bowl. Add 2 tbsp peanut butter and microwave 1 min. Mix well and mold into bottom and sides of bowl to make crust.
Combine rest of peanut butter with cream cheese and sugar. Mix well and heat in microwave 1 min. Stir again and pour into crust.
Let cool and chill on ice 4 hours.
Makes 1 pie - 4 servings.

"Some things worth dying for, are worth living for."
Unknown

Yule Log

Qty.	Description	Commissary #
1 pk	Chocolate Chip Cookies	3215
1 pk	Gingersnaps	3235
4 pks	Duplex Sandwich Cookies	3220
2 tbsp	Baking Soda	3000
40 pkts	Sugar	3490
4 scoops	Lean Meal	3600
8 pks	Cream Cheese	3164
4 scoops	Egg Powder	3610

You will also need:
Plastic 2 ft sq, 3 Bowls, 1 cup

Approx Cost: $13.50 total
$1.70/slice

Separate all of the duplex cookies (like Oreo's) and scrape all the creamy centers into a bowl for use on icing later.
Crush all cookies into a powder in another bowl. Add baking soda and mix well. Set aside
Combine 20 packets of sugar in another bowl with 2 scoops of lean meal. Add 1 cup hot water and mix well. Pour into cookie crumbs and mix well until you have a stiff dough.
Pour dough onto center of plastic and shape into a large square about 10" by 10" by 1/2" thick. (Place plastic on cardboard or something to carry it with) Bake cake in microwave 3-4 min without stirring until dough is firm in the center but not burnt on the edges. (Check often while baking and pause to allow to cool if necessary) Let cake cool 2 hours before proceeding.
Make icing with cookie centers and cream cheese. Add 2 scoops of lean meal and 20 packets of sugar and mix well. You can add cocoa or creamer for flavoring if you like.
Fill tumbler 1/4 with water and add egg powder. Place lid on tumbler and shake egg mixture well. Pour egg mixture into icing mix and mix well. Microwave icing 1-2 minutes stirring every 30 sec until icing is smooth and soft. Pour onto cooled cake and spread evenly. Let cool about 1 hour and roll cake up like a swiss roll spiral. Let cool 2-3 more hours before serving.
Makes about 8 slices.

Variations:
You can add M&M's or peanuts or whatever you like to the mix.

"It won't be true if I don't say it." The Story of Edgar Sawtelle

I would like to take this opportunity to thank you for reading and using my cookbook. I hope you find it useful and entertaining.

Thank you and God bless you!

I would also like to apologize for my crassness in some of my comments concerning cops and our legal justice system. I guess I have become jaded in here and I have seen the corruption in so many cases. I would also like to apologize for my foul language in here. I was going to edit it out but I decided to keep it real. This is prison. I am trying to live for God, and I constantly fall short, but I am still a much better man than I was out there.

Finally I would like to apologize to my family, and especially my kids who have possibly suffered the most in all this. I am truly sorry for what I did, and I am sorry for ending up in prison and abandoning you. I hope someday you can forgive me, but mostly I hope you don't hate me for what I did. Trust in the Lord.

I love you. God bless you!

Now I want to make clear, I do belong here. In fact I turned myself in and confessed my crime. Yeah I did what I've been telling you not to do. Every case is different and in my case, I had to take this route. I'm not sure I agree with my sentence, but I accept it. But I see people every day that I believe were screwed worse than me. And I see the behavior in the cops around me every day. It is a shame that people choose to treat others the way they do. Inmates are people too.

www.ingramcontent.com/pod-product-compliance
Ingram Content Group UK Ltd.
Pitfield, Milton Keynes, MK11 3LW, UK
UKHW041917190726
13854UKWH00003B/1298

9 781105 265341